The Hulsean Lectures for 1907–8

The

Rights and Responsibilities

of

National Churches

T0370678

The

Rights and Responsibilities

of

National Churches

by

J. HOWARD B. MASTERMAN, M.A.

Professor of History in the University of Birmingham
Vicar of S. Michael's, Coventry
Examining Chaplain to the Bishop of Manchester

CAMBRIDGE :

at the University Press

1908

CAMBRIDGE
UNIVERSITY PRESS

University Printing House, Cambridge CB2 8BS, United Kingdom

Published in the United States of America by Cambridge University Press, New York

Cambridge University Press is part of the University of Cambridge.

It furthers the University's mission by disseminating knowledge in the pursuit of education, learning and research at the highest international levels of excellence.

www.cambridge.org
Information on this title: www.cambridge.org/9781107671836

© Cambridge University Press 1908

First published 1908
First paperback edition 2014

A catalogue record for this publication is available from the British Library

ISBN 978-1-107-67183-6 Paperback

To SIR OLIVER LODGE, D.Sc., F.R.S.

PRINCIPAL OF THE UNIVERSITY OF BIRMINGHAM.

I have not asked your leave to associate this book with your name, for by doing so I might seem to be claiming your support for the views therein propounded; yet I am glad of the opportunity of recording my strong conviction that for you, and many who like you are on quest for that assured conviction of truth that can be restored to our perplexed age only through the travail of human souls, our Church has a home and a welcome—a welcome that loyalty to our Lord gives us the right to offer, and that loyalty to truth does not forbid you to accept.

"The fact that religion is becoming increasingly significant as a means of consolation and that this point of view is so strongly emphasized, are signs of its altered position in the spiritual life. Religion was once the pillar of fire which went before the human race in its great march through history, showing it the way. Now it is fast assuming the role of the ambulance which follows in the rear and picks up the exhausted and wounded. But this too is a great work. It is however not sufficient; and when religion has disburdened herself of all her dead values, she will once more, in intimate association with ethics, rise to be a power which leads men forward."

HÖFFDING, *The Philosophy of Religion.*
(English Translation, p. 346.)

PREFACE.

I HAVE thought it best to publish these lectures practically as they were delivered. I have to thank the Rev. J. Neville Figgis for kindly reading them through in MSS. and making several useful suggestions; but he is, of course, in no way responsible for the opinions I have expressed.

It may be well to state shortly the main idea that these lectures are intended to illustrate. It is that Churchmanship and citizenship are the natural expression of the two strongest instincts of humanity —the instinct of self-protection and the instinct of self-sacrifice; that both these instincts find their full scope only under a democratic system; and that the reconciliation of their apparently conflicting claims is to be found in the law of service that finds its fullest expression in the Incarnation.

The question is being asked all round us: Can the English Church meet the needs of the modern world, or is she destined to retreat within ever narrowing frontiers with the advance of the democratic ideal?

Has she, as many believe, lived her life and done her work, or is she, as I believe, at the threshold of a new and larger opportunity of shepherding the nation into the fold of Christ? On the answer to that question depends the future of England.

May God give us His grace that we may know the day of our visitation, lest our house be left unto us desolate.

J. HOWARD B. MASTERMAN.

THE UNIVERSITY,
  BIRMINGHAM.
    February, 1908.

I

THE RELIGIOUS SIGNIFICANCE
OF NATIONALITY.

DANIEL IV. 25.

*Till thou know that the most High ruleth in the kingdom
of men, and giveth it to whomsoever he will.*

Dr Adam Smith has called attention[1] to the influence exercised over the prophets of the eighth century
by the progress of Assyrian conquest. "The old envies
and rancours of the border warfare of Israel with her
foes, which had filled the last four centuries of her
history, are replaced by a new tenderness and compassion towards the national efforts, the achievements
and all the busy life of the Gentile peoples"—"As the
rivalries and hatreds of individual lives are stilled in
the presence of a common death, so even the factious,
ferocious world of the Semites ceased to *fret its anger
and watch it for ever* in face of the universal Assyrian
fear."

The thought is appropriate, for it was in the protest
of the Hebrew prophets against the inexorable march of
the vast inorganic empires of the East that the instinct
of nationality first becomes articulate in world-literature.

[1] Adam Smith, *Book of the Twelve Prophets*, I. 54—5.

It was not individuals, but nations, that the imperialism
of Babylon or Assyria sought to destroy. Rabshakeh's
speech outside the walls of Jerusalem is a summary
of the defence of inorganic imperialism against the
claims of the national spirit. " Make your peace with
me and come out to me ; and eat ye every one of his
vine, and every one of his fig-tree, and drink ye every
one of the waters of his cistern ; until I come and take
you away to a land like your own, a land of corn and
wine, a land of bread and vineyards." To such arguments
of material advantage the only answer lay in an appeal
to the sacredness of the national idea. To the philosophy
of materialism and brute force the Hebrew prophets
oppose the philosophy of history.

"The most High ruleth in the kingdom of men."
To forget that truth is to sink back to the law of
the beast. The Divine sentence on every ruler of men
who ignores the Divine purpose in history is still, " Let
his heart be changed from man's, and let a beast's heart
be given unto him." So Daniel saw in vision

> The giant forms of empires on their way
> To ruin one by one,

till after the brute empires had passed one like a son of
man came near to the Ancient of Days, and the dominion
over all peoples, nations and languages was given to
him. The brute rule of force gives place to the moral
rule of humanity brought near to God.

This consciousness of the sovereignty of God proved

the one adequate safeguard of Jewish national life through ages of exile and oppression. For a time it broadened out, in Amos and Isaiah, into an assertion of the Divine purpose in the history, not of Israel only, but of the nations around. In the growing isolation of the post-exilic life of the nation it becomes narrowed into an assertion of the exclusive vocation of the Jewish nation. The noble protest of the book of Jonah on behalf of a wider interpretation of the purpose of God finds little echo in the Apocalyptic literature in which so much of the Catholic spirit of the great prophets is lost.

The Jewish national instinct, become self-conscious in its contest with the first of the great world-empires, outlasted the repressive efforts of the last and greatest, and has held together a nation deprived of every bond of union but the bond of a common religion and a common hope. Any study of the meaning of nationality must begin with the one nation of the ancient world that remains a nation still.

The nation in later times whose history most nearly resembles that of the Jewish people is the Greek. Dean Church has drawn attention, in his sermons on the Influence of Christianity on National Character, to the effect of a common creed and a common hope in keeping alive the instinct of national life among the Greek people.

" What saved Greek nationality was its Christianity.

It is wonderful that even with it Greek society should have resisted the decomposing forces that were continually at work around it and in it; but without its religion it must have perished. This was the spring of that obstinate tenacious national life which persisted in living on though all things conspired for its extinction; which refused to die under corruption or anarchy, under the Crusader's sword or under the Moslem scimitar."

The disintegration of the last of the great world-Empires was due in part to the influence of Christianity. "Differences of thought and character, which were in abeyance under the Roman rule, began to show themselves again in the modes in which Christianity was apprehended and applied." The settlement of Teutonic tribes within the Empire in the centuries that followed seemed likely to lead to the rise of a group of nations out of the ruin of the Empire in the west. But the imperative need of unity in view of fresh barbarian inroads of Avars, Saracens, Magyars, raised first the Frankish and then the Saxon royal house to the imperial throne, and gave a religious basis to their imperial claims. Only in the lands more sheltered from barbarian attack—in Ireland, England, France—was a national consciousness able to develop. Ireland, remote from the controversies of Western Europe, developed in the sixth century a form of Christian thought and organization that, whatever may have been its weaknesses, was at least distinctively national. Till the storm of Norse invasions broke over Ireland at the end of the eighth century, the Irish Church was, both in learning and in missionary enthusiasm, the pioneer of European progress. In England also the Christian Church was, partly through the instinct of independence infused into it by the northern missionaries, the ally of the national spirit. That Hildebrand hoped to use William the Norman as an agent for denationalizing the English Church is very clear, but the wise policy of William, the struggles of Thomas of Canterbury against Angevin despotism, and the alliance of the Church with the nobles in their efforts to curb the power of John, all tended to keep the English Church in close contact with national life. The Ultramontanism of the fifteenth century came too late to counteract the vast service that the English Church had done in giving a definitely religious sanction to the national aspirations of the English people.

France has passed through a harder and less successful struggle in its efforts to retain a Gallican Church that might give religious expression to its national life. The ultimate victory of Ultramontanism has left French national aspirations without the religious consecration to which the French character is peculiarly fitted to respond.

The Western Church after the time of Gregory the Great looked with growing disapproval on the efforts of the peoples of Europe to assert their national independence. In Germany and Italy, where the contest of the papacy with the national spirit was waged with most success, the great allies of the papacy were the religious orders; its great opponents, the bishops. The Church reform movement that centred in the work of Hildebrand, though in part an effort to prevent the secularization of the Church, was also in part a monastic attack on the tendency of the episcopate to identify itself with the awakening national instinct of the peoples of Western Europe. From that time the struggle of the papacy against the national spirit never ceased. "Herein lay the great contradiction of the mediaeval Church, that which produced its monstrous corruptions. It thought that it could exist without distinct nations, that its calling was to overthrow the nations. Therefore the great virtues which nations foster, distinct individual conscience, sense of personal responsibility, veracity, loyalty, were undermined by it; therefore it called good evil and evil good; therefore it mimicked the nations while it was trampling upon them; therefore it became more bloodthirsty than any nation had ever been[1]."

The Council of Constance marks the beginning of the last effort to reconcile the system of the mediaeval Church with the recognition of the developing ideas of nationality. Yet the Council declared war on the Hussites of Bohemia, whose movement was largely

[1] F. D. Maurice, *Social Morality*, p. 180.

national, as the Pope had declared war on the Albigenses two centuries before. And in the end the attempt to restore the Conciliar authority of the episcopate failed, and the age of Councils is followed by the age of Concordats. At the Council of Trent the Pope withstood all the efforts of Cardinal Pole and others to secure the system of voting by nations that had been adopted at Constance.

The subjugation of the episcopate to the papacy was disastrous in its consequence, for it obliged the national religious aspirations of the peoples of Europe to fall back on the support of the secular sovereign. Marsiglio of Padua prepares the way for the age of Machiavelli and of Luther. Machiavelli is as distinctively the expression of the mind of the Italian Renaissance as Luther is of the German Reformation. Machiavelli, the apostle of efficiency, desired to establish national life on an explicitly non-religious basis; while Luther appealed to the secular princes as the religious leaders of a national Church. The union of the Lutheran tendencies of Cranmer with the Machiavellian policy of Cromwell gave its distinctive character to the early stage of the English Reformation. And even in Spain Philip rather than the Pope was the real head of the Church.

The inevitable reaction followed. The idea of a state-regulated religion is followed by the idea of a religion-regulated state; and Calvinist, Covenanter,

Puritan tried to substitute the despotism of the saints for the despotism of the King. Only in Scotland did this reaction prove successful. There the General Assembly became the real governing body, and the Church gained the strongly national character that it has never since lost. Elsewhere a century of religious wars led on to the general weariness of national and religious enthusiasm that marked the Age of Reason.

The Eastern Church has never accepted the Latin conception of Catholic uniformity. Repudiating the claims of Rome to Latinize her life, she has been able, through the system of Patriarchates, to foster the national life of the peoples whom she has won for the Christian faith. " As the new races in the East were converted, each was allowed to have the divine offices in the vernacular, and each to have its own independent administration, recognizing only the tie of gratitude that bound it in reverence to Constantinople, whose primacy was of honour, not of supremacy[1]."

In Russia, in Greece, in Roumania and the other Balkan states, the policy of the Eastern Church has enabled the instinct of nationality to find a religious sanction. Undoubtedly this has brought with it the danger of the undue subordination of the Church to political influences, and in Russia especially the abolition of the Patriarchate of Moscow in 1823 has led to a condition not unlike the condition of the English Church

[1] See Allen, *Christian Institutions*, ch. x.

under Henry VIII. But in Russia, and among the new nations of Eastern Europe, the Eastern Church has yet a part to play worthy of the greatness of its historic past.

The reawakening of the national idea that began with the French Revolution[1], and has been so marked a characteristic of the Europe of the last century, was the outcome of those ideas of the sovereignty of the people of which Rousseau was the popular exponent, though the origin of them lies much further back in mediaeval scholastic thought. For the sovereignty of the people, if it means anything else than the tyranny of a mere numerical majority—and in Rousseau's conception of it, it never meant that—implies some general mind and will that gives organic character to the state. And this general mind and will is exactly what we mean when we speak of any body of men as a nation. Hence the demand of nations for the right of self-expression— their right to be themselves—becomes a dominant fact in the European history of the nineteenth century. The idea that a state is only in a condition of stable equilibrium when its boundaries coincide with those of a nation, though often hard to apply in practice, may be said to be now almost a commonplace of political thought[2].

[1] The French Revolution, though it began as the expression of an universal brotherhood, gained its real force from the idea of the "Republic, one and indivisible."

[2] See note at end of chapter.

But it is a noteworthy fact that the national spirit has not during the past century been linked with religion. Mazzini alone among the great champions of nationality tried to give a religious character to his crusade for Italian independence. The patriotism of Koskiusko, Kossuth, Cavour, Bismarck, though not without the glamour of romance, is not lightened by the steady gleam of religious consecration. And, indeed, the student of modern history can hardly fail to feel that the old sin—the failure to recognize that the most High ruleth in the kingdom of men—has brought with it a measure of the old penalty—"let his heart be changed from man's, and let a beast's heart be given to him." Divorced from religion, the spirit of nationality becomes aggressive, intolerant, brutal. It asks for the privileges of power without its responsibilities. It forgets that moral worth is the only guarantee for national greatness.

"To me it seems," says Bishop Creighton, "that the differentiation of nations is part of that continuous revelation of God's purpose which is contained in history." The history of the progress of mankind has been the history of the development of two intermediate forms of organized life—the family and the nation—between the individual and the race. The family—with its wider extension in the clan or tribe—belongs to an early stage of civilized life, and has a religious significance so profound that it is probably true to say that Christianity, in fighting for the true ideal of family life, is fighting for what is vital to its own existence.

But what of the nation? The first fact to be noted is, that the nation-making force, as it appears in history, is an ethical force. From the first it makes a claim on human character, to which particular peoples or races are often unable to respond. "The nation-state," says Professor Bosanquet, "as an ethical idea is, then, a faith or a purpose—we might say a mission, were not the word too narrow and too aggressive.... The modern nation is a history and a religion rather than a clear-cut idea. Its power as an idea-force is not known till it is tried[1]."

For not only does a nation live by the subordination of the individual to the collective good, and of the present to the future—it also exists for an ethical purpose. It claims the right to be, not in virtue of the mere blind instinct of survival, but in virtue of some contribution that it deems itself called to make to the cause of humanity. Some sense of vocation, some dimly heard divine call, lies at the heart of every national life. A people that lacks this, lacks the necessary incentive to survival in the midst of contending groups. In the long run, the religious nations will tend to absorb the non-religious nations. Fundamentally, therefore, a nation exists not to get but to give—to keep alive in the world some particular type

[1] Bosanquet, *Philosophical Theory of the State*, p. 321.

of human character or thought. The right of a nation to independence depends on the truth that the life of humanity is enriched through the diversity of national character. For as the Catholic man, which is Christ, is being fulfilled through the diverse gifts that the one Spirit gives to diverse men; so to nations, as to men, the one Spirit divideth severally as He will.

"The claim of a nation to independence"—but how far does the moral obligation to recognize that claim extend? Are there not infant nations that must be trained before they can be set free; and old nations that must be protected, if need be even from themselves? We cannot now accept as a final test the old law that a nation has the right to be independent only if it can show itself strong enough to guard its freedom. Yet the test involves a true principle—the principle that a nation must prove its right to be free at the judgment-bar of humanity by the amount of the sacrifice that it is prepared to make for its freedom. For that sacrifice is the measure of the national consciousness of a divine call, a purpose of God in history that it should be itself. Where a people gives manifest evidence that it intends to use its freedom for purposes of injury to others, or for the oppression of the minority within its borders, that people must be educated in the true meaning of national life, often through the bitter discipline of oppression or exile. For nations need education not less than individuals, and the laws that regulate the relation of nations to each other are still far below the standard of those that regulate the relations of individuals. A man who acted towards his fellow-men as nations habitually act towards each other could not for long be tolerated in any reasonable human society. And the reason for this is, in part, that the elementary rights of the individual are guaranteed to him by the society to which he belongs, while the rights of nations find their only guarantee in the power of each nation to enforce its own. For the sanction of international law lies only in a general moral public opinion that has, as yet, found no effective organ for expressing itself.

It follows from all this that the education of a nation means two things. In the first place it means the training of the people in the exercise of that subordination of private to public good without which the national life cannot maintain itself. Every nation lives by the sacrifice—willing and deliberate, or involuntary and instinctive—that its members offer at the shrine of their common fatherland. The first right that it claims is the right to exist. And therefore the earliest form of organization with which it needs to provide itself is self-protective. And a nation provided with this self-protective organization is what we call a state. Government exists to defend the national life both from internal and external dangers; it claims the goods and services, and if need be the lives, of its citizens in virtue of this paramount need. It is

therefore essential to the true security of the state
that it should provide for its citizens education in the
meaning of citizenship—that it should transform the
vague instinct of patriotism into a clear and conscious
devotion, drawing its inspiration from the records of
the past and the hopes of the future. You will
remember Fichte's noble plea for such education as
the one possible salvation of the German people at the
moment of its deepest humiliation. And the absence
of any adequate sense of this need in our own country
now, should be, to you here to whom the nation looks
for guidance in its educational ideas, a matter of grave
and constant concern.

But a nation exists, not as an end in itself, but as a
means to a larger end—the enrichment of humanity.
It claims the service of the individual citizen in virtue
of a service that it can render to mankind. And
therefore national education involves training in the
collective law of sacrifice; in respect for the rights of
other nations; in that sense of trusteeship the loss
of which left the life of the Jewish people bankrupt
of spiritual power. For to every nation, as truly as to
the Jew, is the old word spoken, " In thy seed shall all
the nations of the earth be blessed." This stage of
national education, whatever name we give to it, is
essentially religious. It is the bringing of the son of
man near to the Ancient of Days that he may receive
dominion founded on the moral law of service.

It follows from what I have said that the state-organization can never express all that the national life exists to contribute to the world. It gives the nation the right to live its own life, it cannot be the vehicle of that life. The beauty of the nation's art, the richness of its thought, the grandeur of its aspirations—these cannot flow through the channels of state-life. They will often find their fullest expression in the life and work of individuals, but they will pass by the process of education into the life of the people, as the general mind comes to see in them the expression of its deepest ideas. National art and national literature are the art and literature to which the national consciousness responds, and which it feels to be the highest expression of its true self.

But most of all, a nation needs the consecration of its mission. And therefore the national spirit has always tried to find for itself a religious sanction. It has asked for a Church that shall come down into its life with the benediction of the Divine, from whose lips it may hear in its own tongue the wonderful works of God. That is what England asked for in its resistance to papal aggressions; that is what France asked for in the Gallican movement, and in the Civil Constitution of the Clergy in the first year of the Revolution; that is what the Hussites of Bohemia and the Albigenses of Aquitaine asked for; what Japan and China are asking for to-day.

The two great enemies of nationality in history

have been Imperialism and the Roman Catholic Church. And in both cases the hostility has sprung from the same cause—distrust in the value of freedom. The Roman Church has been in the past a magnificent foster-mother of nations in their infancy, but she has resented and resisted their efforts to grow into manhood. Her garments are stained with the blood of martyrs who have died in her service; she has carried the light of civilization to peoples sitting in darkness. But she has distrusted the educating power of the Holy Spirit in the life of the nations; she has forgotten that "the most High ruleth in the kingdom of men"; and instead of recognizing the Divine purpose in history she has tried to impose a Divine purpose upon history. Sometimes, surely, she has been found even to fight against God.

For in truth what Rome has tried to impose upon all the nations has not been true Catholicism, but a distinctively local type of Christianity. Italian Christianity may justly claim the respect of every Churchman for the vast services that it has rendered to the cause of Christ. And in the opportunity of consecrating to all noble ends the dawning national life of united Italy, it had a task worthy of its great traditions. But the Roman Church seems to have turned from this, its true task, to pursue the impracticable dream of universal dominion[1].

[1] See Milman, *Hist. of Latin Christianity*, Book III. c. 4.

Yet if in this we impeach the Roman Church, must we not also impeach ourselves? It is impossible to read without deep sorrow the record of the efforts of the English statesmen of the sixteenth century to impose on Ireland a type of Christianity that had been the special product of English genius. Irish Christianity

> Bowed low before the blast
> In patient, deep disdain,

but the outcome of the attempt remains to this day in a religious separation, that has impoverished the world by the loss of the special and peculiar contribution that a national Irish Church, living its own life as a sister Church of our own, might have made to humanity. Nor has the attempt been less disastrous in the case of Scotland, where it shattered all hope of the restoration of the episcopal order in the Presbyterian Church of that country, and resulted in an equally unsuccessful effort to impose a Scottish type of religion on the England of the Commonwealth period.

The spirit of Imperialism, as actually manifested in history, grows out of the spirit of nationality when it has forgotten God. It denies to other peoples the rights that it claims for itself. At its best, it is an attempt to impose the characteristics of one nation on all its subject nations; at its worst, it is simply an attempt to stamp out all varieties of local life in the peoples under its sway. But there is a true Imperialism, towards which our Empire is, we may hope, moving—

an Imperialism that seeks to educate peoples in the lessons of freedom—that takes up "the white man's burden," not for greed or glory, but in the true spirit of nationality which is the spirit of sacrifice. To desire to be the mother of nations is a nobler ambition than to desire to be their conqueror.

The prophet of the Book of Revelation has pictured for us the contest of the nations against the beast of inorganic Imperialism and the false prophet of spurious Catholicism[1], till the coming of the true Kingdom in the light of whose glory the nations shall walk and through whose open gates the glory and honour of the nations shall be brought.

But on the other side, the apparently disintegrating influences of a religion that teaches the supreme and permanent value of the individual life seem at first sight opposed to the national spirit. For nationality implies the subordination of the individual to the general good, while Christianity is irretrievably committed to the doctrine that every individual life has a distinctive value of its own. And, again, Christianity asserts that God "has made of one blood all the nations of men," that in Christ "there cannot be Greek and Jew, circumcision and uncircumcision, barbarian, Scythian, bondman, freeman."

Can a Church pledged to the doctrine of the universal brotherhood of man, and the supreme value

[1] See Renan, *L'Antéchrist*, cxvii.

of each individual life, consecrate with its approval an idea that seems to deny the one and ignore the other?

The first article of the patriotic creed—an article far older than Christianity—is that it is sweet and pleasant to die for one's country; that, in other words, there is no limit to the extent of the claim that patriotism may make on the life of the individual. Patriotism seems to take up the very challenge of Christ, and bid men, if need be, to hate father and mother and wife and children and lands—yea, and their own lives also. Here, then, surely, the Christian man is confronted with two irreconcilable claims—irreconcilable indeed, unless the voice of patriotism be in truth none other than the voice of God; unless the form that stoops over the dying soldier on the battle-field be none other than the form of Christ.

The permanent value of the individual depends on the degree to which all the faculties of his nature have been developed into harmonious activity. And this education only comes as he yields himself to the influences of powers outside his own life, and responds to claims made on him. It is only love expressed in sacrifice that can

> make time break
> And let us pent-up creatures through
> Into eternity, our due.

It is exactly this that patriotism does. It offers an ideal of service wider than the family, and yet not so wide as to be, for most men, practically ineffective. It presents the nation as the larger unit through which the individual may best serve the cause of humanity.

"Not to destroy, but to fulfil" is ever the Divine order. The Divine Father has enriched the life of the individual by setting him in the life of the family, and has enriched the life of the family by setting it in the life of the nation; and has enriched the life of the nation by setting it in the life of humanity.

If this is so, there can be no real antagonism between the claim that Christ makes through His Church and the claim that God makes through national life. The true patriot and the true Christian must somehow mean the same thing. The fact of birth that gives the child its place in the organic life of the nation, and the fact of baptism that gives the child its place in the life of the Christian society, must have some defined relation to each other.

What that relation is we shall be better able to see when we have considered in our next lecture the idea of the Church, but already we can see how deeply the problem we are considering affects the whole course of Christian history. For when we ask for the reconciliation of Churchmanship and patriotism we are really asking for the establishment of the Kingdom of God. The attempt to set up the Kingdom of God as an organized society side by side with, but apart from, other forms of organized life stands condemned at the

bar of history. For if, as is beyond doubt true, the
Eastern Churches and the English Church, in recognizing the religious significance of national life, have
become too political, and have sometimes subordinated
the eternal protest for righteousness, for which the
Church exists, to the exigencies of the moment; the
Roman Church has not, by her contest against national-
ism, escaped the same danger. She has become the
rival of the nations whose teacher she might have been;
she has refused to France and to Italy the consecration
of their national aspirations, and has placed her
children in those lands in the same cruel predicament
as that in which she placed the English adherents of
the old faith in the reign of Elizabeth. And therefore the control of the future is passing out of her
hands. She will not perish, for she is a part of the
Church of Christ, but it may be that in her too the
vision of the prophet may be fulfilled, and the tree
that reached unto heaven, and the sight thereof to the
end of the earth, may have but the stump of its roots
in the tender grass of the field, till she shall learn that
service, not dominion, is the mark of the Church of
Christ, and that the most High ruleth in the kingdom
of men not to destroy but to fulfil.

But to whom will the shaping of the future fall?
The nation-making forces are still at work. A genera-
tion ago Italy and Germany and the smaller peoples of
the Eastern Europe were claiming their place in the

family of nations. To-day it is Japan and China and
Persia, and ere long it will be the colonies that Great
Britain has trained in the power of self-government.
Are we moving slowly towards some vast Armageddon—
the twilight of the nations of the old Norse Sagas?
Or are we watching the dawning of the great day
when that kingdoms of the world shall become the
kingdoms of our God and of His Christ?

On the birthday of the Christian society, the first
sign of the dawn of a new age, was that men of diverse
nations heard, each in his own language, the wonderful
works of God. For the Incarnation was the witness of
God's purpose that the message of heaven should be
spoken in the languages of earth, and the Holy Spirit
in the Christian society carries on from age to age
the gracious purpose of the Father. The words of
S. Paul may surely without irreverence be applied to
our Lord Himself, "To the Jews I became as a Jew
that I might gain Jews." And still the Catholic
manhood of Christ clothes itself in the forms of each
national life, asking of each nation the contribution
that He has fitted it to make to the fulfilment of the
great purpose.

Where Christ goes before, His Church must follow.
Wherever the awakening of a national consciousness
shows that the "hands, that reach through darkness,
moulding men" are still at work in the world, there is
a fresh challenge to the Church of Christ. Again she

is face to face with the mystery of the birth of a spiritual organism; again our Lord is setting a little child in the midst of her.

A nation that does not receive the Gospel of the Incarnation translated into its own language will either construct a religion of its own, or lose the higher ideals of service in mere lust of dominion—the beast-life of the prophet's vision. The religion that a nation makes for itself may incorporate much of the Christian faith, it may accept the Bible as a moral textbook, it may strive after high ideals. But it will lack the note of Catholicity; it will not lift up the nation's life with the inspiring power of a historic faith. It may even become a mere religion of self-assertion, and give a moral sanction to the worst aggressions on the rights of humanity. It may sanction slavery and justify injustice, and glorify war, till the nobler instincts of men rise against it. The religion of a nation that has repudiated its relation to the Catholic Church will almost inevitably come to be a device for strengthening the authority of the dominant power in the state; the note of challenge will die out of its voice; it will be slow to condemn and quick to condone. It may tend at last to preach contentment with things as they are, and become the enemy of progress and aspiration and hope.

Patriotism and Churchmanship—the sense of responsibility, gladly accepted, to the national life, and the sense of responsibility, gladly accepted, to the whole

great body and brotherhood of the Christian Church—
these are the two influences in human life that have
proved themselves strong enough to lift men above
greed and self-interest and all ignoble things. Separated, they confuse human life with a sense of divided
allegiance, and when life's noblest things are in contest
life's ignoble things prosper. Prolong the contest, and
the whole moral fibre of the nation's life is weakened;
the lust of personal gain usurps the place of the passion
for the common good; prosperity brings demoraliza-
tion; and He Who wept over Jerusalem watches again
the tragedy of

> One task more declined, one more footpath untrod,
> One more devil's-triumph and sorrow for angels,
> One wrong more to man, one more insult to God.

There is no sin that more inevitably brings its own
punishment than the putting asunder what God has
joined together.

But patriotism that has behind it all the force of
the Catholic faith would be a regenerating power
lifting up the lives of nations to God. It would
glorify civic service with the light of high idealism, it
would change the voter's question "What shall I get"
into the question "What can I give"; over frontiers
now bristling with bayonets, hands would be stretched
out in a new rivalry of brotherhood; the light that
dawned long ago to lighten the Gentiles would shine at
last into eyes grown dim with long waiting. The

peasant of Armenia or Macedonia; the black serf hounded to death in the Congo forests in the name of European civilization; the men who go under in the strife of modern industrialism because the nations have forgotten wherein lies their true wealth; all these are waiting for the coming of the nations Christian not in name only but in deed and in truth. Of the tree of life that grows in the paradise of God it is written, "The leaves of the tree were for the healing of the nations."

NOTE.

In an Essay on "Nationality" in a recently published volume of Essays, Lord Acton traverses the view that the boundaries of a state should coincide with those of a nation. But he treats nationality entirely as a racial product, whereas in reality many of the strongest nationalities, *e.g.* France and England, are the outcome of a great admixture of races, fused into one in the discipline of history. In actual fact, it is hard to decide whether it is more true to say that the state makes the nation, or that the nation makes the state. Peoples brought by the "accidents of history" under a common government may gradually grow into a nation. Where they fail to do so, as in Austro-Hungary, instability is inevitable and ultimate disruption almost certain. Hence Professor Lavisse defines nationality as "the work of history ratified by the will of man."

II

THE IDEA OF THE CHURCH.

REV. XXI. 10.

*He showed me the holy city Jerusalem, coming down
out of heaven from God.*

Two truths are implied in this vision of the prophet.
Firstly, it is implied that there is a Divine Order in the
spiritual world, a Kingdom of the Heavens where the
Will of God is done. And secondly, it is implied that
this Divine Order is in process of being fulfilled through
the coming down of the supernatural into the world of
men.

There is a Kingdom of the Heavens. The denial of
this involves the assumption that there are no other
beings in the universe with intelligence and will. But
it involves more. It involves the denial of any real
meaning to human life. For unless the dead pass into
a Divine Order for which human life has been a prepara-
tion religion has no adequate meaning and life no
adequate purpose.

That there is such a Divine Order is a central truth
in the teaching of our Lord. Sometimes He spoke of it
as a kingdom of which God was king; sometimes as a

family of which God was father; sometimes as a flock of which God was shepherd. But He always spoke of it as the most real of all things, for the Will of God is the supreme reality of the universe, and Heaven means the condition where the Will of God is perfectly done.

But He also spoke of the Kingdom of the Heavens as coming down into the world of men. So that the name sometimes seems to stand in His teaching for the unseen Divine Order where the Will of God is perfectly done; sometimes for the imperfect counterpart of that Divine Order as it grows up in the world of men. For the result of the earthly life of Christ was the establishment of a society of men pledged to the doing of the Will of God on earth as it is done in heaven. The Church came into existence to raise the natural to the standard of the supernatural, to bring the human into conformity with the Divine.

It is necessary to insist on this as essentially involved in the idea of the Church, in view of modern proposals to give the name of Church to forms of organization from which the idea of the supernatural is explicitly excluded.

Sir John Seeley's *Natural Religion* is the best and most eloquent exposition of the view that regards the Christian Church as "simply the spiritual side of the great organism of civilized society throughout the Western world," and appeals for the abandonment of supernaturalism as a merely accidental feature of religion.

The same view has been attractively presented in Dr Stanton Coit's recently published volume on *National Idealism and a State Church*. If by the abandonment of supernaturalism is meant that the Church's work lies in the actual world of men and that its task is to fit men for heaven by making them good citizens of earth ; or if it be meant that the Church must cease to set the supernatural in opposition to the natural, and must recognize that it is the same God who is revealed in the uniformities of nature and in the Incarnation ; then the protest against a false Supernaturalism is timely and wise. But if it is meant that out of the spiritual world that we call Heaven there comes, and can come, no help or guidance to men, then we must reply that if this is true the very idea of the Church ceases to have any meaning. For not only do truth and righteousness mean, in the Church's idea, the correspondence of the human mind and will to the Divine Order, they also imply that that Order is by the action of the Holy Spirit entering into and lifting up human life.

What then is the Church ? It is a society of men organized for the purpose of realizing the Divine ideal under the actual conditions of human life. And it follows that, ideally, the Church is coextensive with humanity. For the Church is humanity organized in accordance with the Will of God. "The Church," says F. D. Maurice, "is human society in its normal state, the world the same society irregular and abnormal. The world is the Church without God; the Church is the world restored to its relation with God, taken back by him into the state for which he created it[1]."

In the sacrament of infant baptism the Christian society asserts the fact that membership of the Church belongs to the normal idea of human life. Every man has the right to belong to the Christian society unless by his own act he has willed otherwise.

But as a member of the society he is presented with a certain standard of belief and conduct which the society sets before its members as the true ideal. A creed and a commandment are delivered to him.

First, a creed. For the confession that Jesus Christ is Lord, Son of God and Saviour of the world, lies at the foundation of the life of the Christian society. It is the duty of every Churchman to resist, strenuously if need be, the attempt to treat the Christian Creed as a series of propositions to be assented to or denied in detail[2]. The Christian Creed is a statement of what

---

[1] *Theological Essays*, p. 343.

[2] I am referring here to the qualification for membership of the Christian society, not to the qualifications of those who are to be the teachers of that society. No University would exclude a student from admission to its ranks because he believed *Magna Carta* to be a forgery of the fourteenth century; though such a belief might be held to be a disqualification for appointment as a Professor of History. Yet an

the conscience of the Christian society has felt to be implied in the Lordship of Christ. It is the framework that protects the central truth that we believe in Jesus Christ His only Son, our Lord. The Church is built on one rock, not a series of disconnected pinnacles.

And as the Christian man is bound to resist the attempt to transform his Creed from a living whole into a collection of dissected fragments; so he must resist the efforts of any particular age to add to the credenda of the Christian society. For the Christian Creed is not a yoke of bondage but a Charter of Liberty. It imposes a barrier against all the efforts of men to give to some temporary phase of thought the name of Catholic truth.

Such dangers are constantly present. The Roman Church, caught in the meshes of a particular philosophical theory, has entangled herself in the dogma of Transubstantiation; and Scottish religious life has found it no easy task to shake itself free from the Calvinistic formulae imposed on it by an earlier age. Particular theories of the Atonement, particular views of inspiration, have from time to time been set up as part of the credenda of the Christian Church. But

University that made it a necessary qualification that its teaching staff should avow their specific assent to every accepted conclusion in their respective subjects, would not be likely to contribute much to the advancement of human thought. Willingness to learn and a great passion for truth are at least as important as qualifications for a teacher as orthodoxy of opinion.

the Catholic heart of the Christian society returns always to the one truth that she loves, the one truth that gives stability to human hope and value to human effort.

And as the belief of the Christian society centres round one truth—the truth of the Lordship of Christ, so its ethical standard centres round one law—the law of love. It finds the ethical teaching of its sacred books briefly comprehended in this one saying: Thou shalt love thy neighbour as thyself. It is by its conformity to that standard that the Christian society of any age or nation proves itself a part of the great brotherhood. In vain will any society plead the continuity of its orders, the validity of its sacraments, if the issue be not manifestly seen in the spirit of love. "For the fruit of the Spirit is love, joy, peace, long-suffering, gentleness, goodness, faith, meekness, temperance." Better, far better, a mutilated body that has life, than a body with all its members well formed and complete—but dead.

It is this ethical test of Catholicity that we need to keep constantly before us if we desire to retain a due sense of proportion in the controversies of our own time. For the true unity of the Church is the unity of mutual love. And therefore unity must be first an instinct before it can become a fact. The deepest of all unities, the unity of the Godhead itself, is the unity of infinite love. And it was this unity that our Lord set before

His Church as its true ideal. It is not the disunion
among the Churches of Christ to-day that most clearly
shows how far they have fallen below the standard of
the Divine ideal; it is the contented acquiescence in
disunion. For if the Church is the Body of Christ,
every member of that dismembered body must ache to
be reunited. True Catholicism is a great passion for
the ingathering of all men once more into the great
society. It is the yearning of the Holy Spirit for the
fulfilment of His purpose of love. It is the throb of
the very heart of God.

Ideally, then, the Church is a universal brotherhood,
held together by belief in the one central truth of the
universe—the truth of the Incarnation ; and seeking to
fulfil the one central law of the universe—the law
of love.

But if there is to be such a brotherhood in the
world, it must find some organized expression, it must
possess some guarantee for the continuity of its life.
For brotherhood has no meaning unless there is the
common life of the family in which it expresses itself.
Members of the Christian society must somehow be
able to feel that they belong to each other.

Yet if the Christian brotherhood becomes an organized society side by side with, and apart from, other
forms of social organization a kind of dualism grows up,
ending in a compromise in the life of the individual
Christian between the claims of the Church on the one

side, and the family and nation on the other. The two citizenships remain dissociated, and life is impoverished by that which is designed to enrich it. It was this dualism that shattered the mediaeval Church, as it had helped to shatter the Roman Empire ages before.

In his description of the day of Pentecost, S. Luke claims as the special sign of the new age that the Divine Spirit is poured out, no longer on a few elect souls, but on sons and daughters, servants and handmaids. The glory of the new brotherhood lay in this, that it was a brotherhood of the poor, a society for the common people.

In the records of the ministry of our Lord Jesus Christ, a prominent feature is His recognition of the point of view of the ordinary man. In marked contrast to the contempt of the professional religious teachers for the people "that knoweth not the law," He is represented as drawing out men's ideas, and listening patiently to their opinions. He founded his kingdom on unconquerable belief in the essential goodness of the human heart. He believed in men because He loved them ; and because he believed in them and trusted them, He called out all the secret forces of good in them. He taught men to know their own sinfulness by showing them what human life might be.

And through all the early period of the history of the Church, the fundamentally democratic character of the new brotherhood persisted. The executive authority of the episcopate rested on the general support of the brotherhood. For the living voice of the Holy Spirit spoke through the mind and conscience of the whole society. Heresies grew up for the most part out of the inordinate influence of individual teachers, but the general mind of the Church remained sound. Gnosticism might attempt to establish the rule of an intellectual aristocracy, but the Church would have none of it.

But to say that the Christian Church is fundamentally democratic does not mean that the mere vote of a numerical majority at any given moment is the supreme court of appeal for all questions. We need to keep in mind Rousseau's distinction between the General Will and the Will of All. "The General Will aims at a common interest; and it is this community of interest, and not the number of votes in which it may find expression, which in truth generalizes the Will. The Will of All aims at private interest as such, and is only a sum of particular wills." "The distinction," says Professor Bosanquet, "between such a sum of wills, and a will that aims at a truly common interest or good, rests upon the fundamental contrast between a mere aggregate and an organic unity[1]."

The Church can never be a mere organization for enforcing the decisions of the numerical majority of the

[1] Bosanquet, *Philosophical Theory of the State*, p. 112.

moment. An Athanasius may at any given moment stand almost alone, and yet prove in the end to have been the true representative of the general mind and will. For an organic society must have a continuous life and character of which its members at any particular moment are only imperfectly conscious. To quote Professor Bosanquet again, "The habits and institutions of any community are, so to speak, the standing interpretation of all the private wills which compose it, and it is thus possible to assign to the General Will an actual and concrete meaning as something different at once from every private will, and from the vote of any given assembly, and yet as standing, on the whole, for what both the one and the other necessarily aim at sustaining as the framework of their life[1]." In the Christian society, this General Will, seeking the good of each in the good of the whole, and expressing the deeper self of the society, is, so the Church believes, none other than the voice of the Holy Spirit. And the supreme purpose of all Church organization should be to give to this voice an adequate vehicle for the utterance of itself. If what I have said already is true, this vehicle will not be found through the gradual restriction of the work of government and guidance in the Christian society to an inner circle of trained officials, but in the widening of the sense of responsibility among all the members of the body.

[1] Bosanquet, *Philosophical Theory of the State*, p. 123.

This idea of the Christian society has been preserved in the Eastern Church much more clearly than in the West. "The Eastern Church, and especially the Russian, considers that to the whole body of the Church—laity as well as clergy—belongs the Divine Spirit, working through faith and love, which preserves the Church from error. This fact is brought out by the extent to which the religious life of the people never requires, as so often in this country, to be kept alive by the energy of the clergy[1]."

But a democratic society must have organs for giving effect to the general mind and will. Such executive organs may vary in character, in method of appointment, in the extent of their powers—the one essential thing is that they shall represent and give effect to the mind and will of the whole society.

And, as part of this task, they may rightly be entrusted with the work of keeping the society true to itself—appealing from the whim of the moment to the deeper and more permanent will of the community. In them the past and the future may claim their right to be heard at the judgment bar of the present.

Yet the ultimate responsibility must rest upon the whole society. The strongest argument for a democratic system either in Church or State is its unique educational value, and this educational value depends

---

[1] Headlam, *The teaching of the Russian Church*, p. 28. See also Birkbeck, *Russia and the English Church*, I. 94.

on the degree to which the community is not in leading-strings but free. The ideal Church is the Church where every member is conscious of his responsibility for the well-being of the whole body, where the defence and interpretation of truth is felt to be the concern of all, where each brings his own particular gift to the common life of the society.

In the world of politics the chief enemy of democracy is bureaucracy. For a bureaucratic state is a state that has lost its organic character—where everything is done for the people, nothing by the people. And the more efficient a bureaucracy shows itself, the more completely the political education of the people is stifled. So, in the Christian society, the real enemy of the organic life of the Church has been the growth of an official class claiming an independent source of authority as lords over God's heritage.

The bureaucratic spirit in the political world is fostered especially by two influences—the influence of official immunities and the influence of centralization. The system established by Napoleon in France is perhaps the most typical example of a bureaucracy in modern Europe. That system was established on two principles. In the first place, all authority was derived from the central power, and all officials were taught to feel their responsibility to Napoleon himself; in the second place, every official was protected by a special administrative law that removed him from the control of the ordinary law courts. It cannot be denied that Napoleon provided France with a strikingly efficient administrative system, but it was a system under which many of the best qualities of national life decayed. A bureaucratic system means the sacrifice of education to efficiency. A bureaucratically governed nation may gain the whole world, but it will lose its own soul.

The British system of government is probably the least bureaucratic of any system of modern Europe. And the reasons for this are, firstly, that officials are generally appointed by and responsible to the general body of citizens, and secondly that no special *droit administratif* protects the official from responsibility to the ordinary law. We value both these principles of English life not because they make for efficiency, but because they make for what we prize more than efficiency, the education of the citizen in the consciousness of responsibility.

But what bearing has all this on the idea of the Church ? This, that the bureaucratic tendency in the Christian society has been fostered by the same causes. The development of a centralized authority claiming for itself the control of the clergy, and the development of special courts and codes of law for the clergy—these have been the influences that have done most to foster that spirit of bureaucracy that is so often attacked under the mistaken title of sacerdotalism.

For, in truth, bureaucracy is the enemy of true sacerdotalism, and mimics the characteristics of the good that it destroys.

For true sacerdotalism asserts the representative character of the *sacerdos*. It behoves every true priest to be made "in all points like unto his brethren." Whatever promotes the isolation of the clerical order, whatever tends to establish a different moral standard for the clergy and the laity, whatever tends to substitute the idea of authority for the idea of service as the ideal of the ministerial life, is the outcome of the bureaucratic spirit. Surely it was not for nothing that our Lord reiterated His warnings against the danger of introducing into the Christian society ideas of lordship or authority. The true priest is the man who stands for the Christian society by its own will and choice, in whose person the local Christian community offers to the service of the whole Church of Christ the special gift that it has to give.

But the Christian society is one; and the call of the local Church must be ratified by the whole body. That is the essential truth that underlies the episcopal system. The Will of the Holy Spirit is expressed through the appointed agents of the entire Christian society.

It does not fall within the scope of this lecture to discuss the question of what constitutes valid ordination. All that I am exercised to do now is to lay stress on the fact that, as " He who crowns himself is not the more, kingly," so he who sets himself up as a priest is not the more priestly.

It belongs to the idea of the Church that it should be a self-governing body—self-governing because the Holy Spirit of Christ dwells in the whole body as the true source of its life. And self-government implies the right to create the executive organs through which the whole body acts.

At the centre of the life of the Church is the sacrament of Holy Communion. For the sacrament of Holy Communion is the perpetual witness of her fundamentally democratic character. Here the simplest and most universal human need becomes the bond of union of a universal brotherhood. May I not plead here, in the name of the Catholic ideal of the Church, against the attempt now being made to interpret a rubric of our Prayer Book in such a way as to exclude from the rights of Christian fellowship men whose baptism our Church acknowledges, and who are at one with us in the fundamentals of our creed. The whole instinct of the Christian society, where she is true to her mission, is not exclusive but inclusive. It is only the sectarian spirit that excludes. The Christian brotherhood must not sit with barred doors guarding the wedding feast from all but the invited guests; it must go out and gather in as many as it can find, both bad and good, that the wedding may be furnished with guests. When the King comes in to see the guests, He will know how to speak to men's consciences the old question, "Friend, how camest thou in hither, not having on a wedding garment?" I am sure that we need to beware lest, in seeking to defend our holy things from unworthy hands, we narrow down "by false limits of our own" the Catholic invitation of Christ. However emphatically we assert, as we may most truly assert, the value of the ceremony of Confirmation, by which the Christian man confesses his need of the Divine Spirit and receives the gift of fuller life; still, nothing can justify the Christian society in saying to any man "By your baptism in the name of the triune God you belong to the great brotherhood— no unwillingness on your part to recognize the fact can make it other than true. You are within the Catholic Church, however irregular may have been the mode of your entry. Yet at our Catholic altar you shall have no place, in our holy things you shall have no share." By his own act, or by hereditary influences, a man may find himself a non-conforming member of the Catholic Church. But the Catholic Church must keep for him a place and a welcome. He must know that there is no good thing that she has to give that is not his if he will but claim it.

I plead for this, because I want to see Holy Communion once more the bond of union of a universal brotherhood. I dream sometimes of the day when the diverse religious bodies in this land of ours, without laying aside their distinctive character, shall meet at the Holy Communion as the assertion of the fundamental unity of those who serve the one Lord, whose most real presence is made known to us still in the breaking of bread.

Lastly, the Church is that form of organization in which the life of the individual most fully attains itself. For it is in the Christian society that the individual is brought into conscious relation with the ultimate purpose of God. In the family and the nation the individual is trained in the habit of loyalty and self-forgetfulness and sacrifice for common ends. But the Church looks forward further than family or nation. Still, as of old, she is "looking for and earnestly desiring the coming of the day of God"; she is the guardian and trustee of the world's hope; she is ever going forth to meet the bridegroom. And therefore she is the friend of progress, the enemy of timidity and stagnation. She knows that the Divine Purpose will not fail; as she prays "Thy Kingdom come," she knows that God is even now answering her prayer.

"The friend of progress?" But shall we not be reminded that the Eastern Church boasts that it has changed nothing for a thousand years? Shall we not be reminded of Galileo in the dungeons of the Inquisition, and of recent Papal Encyclicals against modern thought? Shall we not be told of our own

Church in league with Stuart reaction or suspicious of popular reform in later times.

It is true. Yet the Church has been the half-unconscious leader of the progress that she has suspected and disowned. There would have been no Galileo if she had not for ages been training the imagination of men ; there would have been no doctrine of the sovereignty of the people if she had not taught for ages that every man had his value with God. But the tragedy of the life of the Church has been that she has not recognized the Master's footsteps as He has come to her along the corridors of history, and has incurred so often the old rebuke "O, thou of little faith, wherefore didst thou doubt ?"

And yet the hope of the world is still in her keeping. For she alone can give to the aspirations of men the guarantee for lack of which effort flags and hearts grow weary.

My brethren, I would gladly, if I could, awaken in your minds a stronger enthusiasm for the idea of the Church. We who are students of history find ourselves so often obliged to investigate the pathology of an organism that seems sick unto death. It is rent with schisms, it is corrupted with worldliness. It fights with carnal weapons and intrigues with sinful ingenuity. It bends its neck to the world's yoke; it wears soft clothing in kings' palaces. Yet behind all the compromise and corruption, it lives. Still, in its darkest

days, the Bread is broken at its altars, and the Lordship of Christ is confessed in its creeds. It lives
because it is the expression of an idea without which
humanity cannot grow to its full stature—because men
cannot do without it.

Yet it is the measure of the failure of the Christian
Church that men are even now blind to the reality of
their need. Recent controversies in the political world
have brought home to us all the degree to which the
idea of religion has become dissociated from the idea
of an organized society. Religion that must not express itself in the language used by any Christian
society, that may not offer to the spiritual aspirations
of men the shelter of a home, the welcome of a
brotherhood—can we dare to hope that such a religion
will have the strength to withstand the forces arrayed
against it?

Therefore we must return again to the idea of the
Church. We must see it as the incarnate expression
of the compassion of God; the body and bride of
Christ. We must see it, in dreams, going out to every
man who is trying to follow Christ to say to him " You
are one of us. All that we have is yours; our love to
sustain you; our hope to assure you ; our altars to feed
you." We must see it as it leaps to the challenge of
selfishness and greed, with the cry of the Magnificat
on its lips: "He hath put down the mighty from
their seat; and hath exalted the humble and meek."

We must see it lifting up into new meaning the life of the family and the nation. We must see it passing on the men whom it has trained for the life of heaven to "the general assembly and Church of the firstborn."

Can these things be? Or must they remain for ever only a wonderful dream out of which we awake to the old solitary nothingness?

That is the challenge that we must answer. It is the unconscious challenge of all the social forces that are awakening in men a new restlessness and a new hope. May we not say, in the words of Milton, "Now once again by all concurrence of signs and by the general instinct of holy and devout men, as they daily and solemnly express their thoughts, God is decreeing to begin some new and great period in his Church?" "A little generous prudence, a little forbearance with one another, and some grain of charity might win all these diligences to join and unite into one general brotherly search after truth [1]."

[1] *Areopagitica.*

III

NATIONAL CHURCHES AND THE
CATHOLIC CHURCH.

MATT. XXVIII. 19, 20.

Go ye therefore, and make disciples of all the nations, baptizing them into the name of the Father and of the Son and of the Holy Ghost: teaching them to observe all things whatsoever I commanded you: and lo, I am with you alway, even unto the end of the world.

So the early Church conceived of her work, not as the gathering of a few elect souls out of the ruins of human society, but as the uplifting of human society through the transforming power of the name of Christ. Her commission was to make disciples of all the nations, bringing to them a new sacramental grace and a new ethical standard. And this transformation was not to be effected by imposing on all men the racial characteristics of the nation in which Christianity was born. The great contest that followed the beginning of the evangelization of the Gentiles was a contest between the advocates of this view and those who, like S. Paul, claimed for the nations the right to enter the Christian society without the surrender of

their national customs and characteristics. The decision of the Council of Jerusalem, while recognizing
the Christian duty of mutual consideration, definitely
decided against the attempt to confine Catholic Christianity within the framework of the Jewish religious
system. But it did more. It made the first attempt
to build up for the Church a body of Catholic regulations. Abstinence from idolatry, personal purity of
character, and respect for the sacredness of life[1]—these
are the great elementary principles of Christian conduct
that every Gentile Church was charged to observe. But
as the Christian society increased, other regulations
grew up in the Churches of the Christ, to which
S. Paul could appeal against the contentiousness of
individual opponents of his authority[2]. And while the
mission of the Church was to a world where local
custom was everywhere breaking down under the
influence of all-pervading Greek culture and all-
controlling Roman law, no wide divergence of local
custom was likely to arise.

But when the uniformity of the Empire was finally
shattered by the inroads of the barbarians, the problem
of the early Church returned in a new form and on a
wider scale. The question at issue was not now, should
the Gentile be obliged to keep the law of Moses, but,
should the Teuton and the Slav be compelled, as a
condition of entry into the Christian society, to submit

[1] Hort, *Judaistic Christianity*, pp. 68—71.   [2] 1 Cor. xi. 16.

to the decrees and customs of the Roman Church.
The wise liberality of Gregory the Great was abandoned in the centuries that followed, and no S. Paul
arose to claim again the freedom of the nations. I
have traced in an earlier lecture the outcome of this;
my only object in referring to it now is to point out
how the Church of the first century gave to the nations
a freedom that the Roman Church of the tenth century
denied them.

I ask you to-day to consider the relation of national
Churches to the Catholic Church. I said in an earlier
lecture that a nation may embody its religious consciousness in an organized institution that shall be
self-contained, and unrelated to any body outside itself.
Such an organization may claim the title of a national
Church, but it will repudiate the right of any authority
outside itself to impose any restrictions on its action.
With a national Church of this kind I am not concerned in these lectures. For I have tried to show
that the idea of the Church involves the conception
of the life of a nation brought into relation to something larger and more lasting than itself—that it is
the reaching out of national life towards the larger
life of humanity.

As a matter of history, no Church grows up as an
unrelated national institution. For Christian truth
is propagated by the accredited agents of existing
Churches. The evangelization of a nation means the

bringing of the nation into religious communion with some existing Christian society. It is only in our own age that the experiment of undenominational missions has been tried, and there is no reason to believe that they are likely to be a permanent phase of Christian activity.

At first the dependence of the new Church on its parent-society must be very close. From this parent-society it will receive its teachers, forms of worship, and methods of organization. There will therefore be an exotic element in the life of a new Church, for the parent-society will itself have a national character. Irish Christianity did not lay aside its special characteristics when it evangelized the north of England, nor could Augustine, at Canterbury, shake himself sufficiently free from the traditions of his native Rome to carry out fully the policy recommended by Gregory. The English Church cannot cease to be English in China or India, nor the Roman Church to be Roman in Japan or in Africa.

But as the Church takes root in a new soil its local characteristics change. It brings forth sons able to guide it, it begins to speak a language of its own, to interpret the Christ in relation to its own conditions and needs. And at this stage there comes the danger lest in repudiating the local characteristics of the parent-society, the young Church may separate itself from the whole family of Churches, may demand the portion of goods that falls to it, and go forth in search of a place where it may live its own life without the restraints that belong to the catholic life of the Father's house.

For Catholicity means a relation between Churches like that which exists between the members of one family, or the states of one empire.

Let us examine these analogies more in detail. Every national Church has, so to speak, a Christian name and a surname—a name that marks it out as a member of a family, and a name that expresses its distinctive individual character. So the title " English Church " conveys a much truer thought than " Church of England," for it tells us of a local society that claims to belong to the great family of Churches, that persists in that claim even though it is repudiated by other members of the family.

The bond that holds together a family is the bond of common ancestry, common traditions and interests, the instinct of a common life. It is something much deeper than conscious, deliberate choice, something that persists, even when all the obligations it involves are repudiated, something that even among the swine-troughs stirs the deep, primitive instincts of the human heart, till it becomes a voice and a resolve, " I will arise, and go to my Father."

It is this instinct that calls Christian societies out of their isolation back to the family life of the Churches of the Christ. It does not formulate terms of reunion or haggle over the relative degree of responsibility for the disunion of the past; it claims its right, its inalienable right, to come back to the Father's house.

But it is the same instinct that, in the Father's house, keeps watch for the returning exile. The attitude of the elder brother of the parable is as real a repudiation of the life of the family as that of the prodigal. The catholic spirit does not cavil over conditions of recognition—the ring and the best robe come afterwards—it goes out to meet the returning exile a great way off. It does not boast of its Catholicity, of the orthodoxy of its formulas, or the continuity of its obedience—it is Godlike in its self-forgetfulness.

We may think of national Churches as brothers in one family. But we may also think of them as states in one Empire. And as the first of these analogies helps us to understand what the catholic spirit is; so the second helps us to understand how the catholic spirit may embody itself in the organized forms of national Church life.

Notice first that there is no such thing as a British Empire apart from the states that compose it. Every British subject is a citizen of the Empire because he is a citizen of his own particular state in the Empire. As an Englishman, a Canadian, an Australian, he shares in all the rights of imperial citizenship. The Canadian cannot repudiate his Canadian citizenship, and yet remain a citizen of the Empire. And just as Canada is, for the Canadian, the local embodiment of the Empire, so the English Church is, for the Christian Englishman, the local embodiment of the Catholic Church. Of course a colony can repudiate its relation to the Empire, as the New England colonies did at the time of the Declaration of Independence. But the English Church has never repudiated its relation to the Catholic Church; it has denied the right of a sister-Church to usurp authority over the whole family, but in that very denial there is implied a denial of the right of that sister-Church to decree its expulsion from the family.

The British Empire, as it grows, will be obliged to recognize more and more the right of appeal from the British home government to the whole Empire, and this appeal, if made, would be exactly analogous to the appeal made by the English Church at the Reformation —an appeal to which she still adheres.

But what is really involved in the relation of a national Church to the catholic society? Here, again, the analogy of the British Empire will help us. For the Empire is held together by three bonds of union—the authority of the Crown, exercised by accredited agents in every part of the Empire; the common law which is deemed to exist in every part of the Empire, except where it has been specifically changed in any particular colony; and the prohibition that restrains any colonial legislature from making laws "repugnant to the laws of England."

Let us examine these three points more in detail.

1. The common authority of the Crown, exercised through accredited agents. At the present stage in the development of the Empire it is usual to send colonial governors from the home-country, but already there is a strong feeling in the self-governing colonies that distinguished colonial leaders should be selected as representatives of the Crown. Indeed, there is no reason why the Governors of our great self-governing colonies should not be elected by the colonies. For one part of the function of the Colonial Governor is to represent the feelings and ideas of the colony to the Crown. But as the other part of his function is to represent the authority of the Crown in the affairs of the colony, he must receive his right to act from the central authority. He may be nominated by the colony, but he must be appointed by the Crown. You see already how closely analogous such a position is to that of a bishop in a national Church. For a bishop is the defender of the interests of the Catholic Church in the life of the local society, and also the representative of the local society in the counsels of the Catholic Church. But just at this point the analogy becomes imperfect, for while the authority of the Crown permeates the Empire as an impersonal influence, the King of the Christian society is not

localized, but omnipresent. The bishop is not the representative of an absent Christ, but the organ of a present Christ, who dwells for ever with His people.

2. The common law of the Empire. "As in the case of a settled colony the Englishman takes his law with him, the fundamental law, or, as English lawyers would say, the common law, of every such colony is the English law as existing at the time of the settlement, or as modified by subsequent legislation of the Imperial Parliament, expressly or by necessary implication extending to that colony[1]." As a new colony starts life, as it were, with a body of law derived from the parent-state, but liable to be modified by subsequent local action, so a national Church starts life with an inheritance of tradition and custom that it must be deemed to retain except in so far as it may be modified by subsequent action[2]. Such action may take the

---

[1] Sir Henry Jenkyns, *British Rule and Jurisdiction beyond the Seas*, p. 6.

[2] " The controversy as to how far the Canon Law was recognized in England, in which Bishop Stubbs and Professor Maitland are sometimes said to have taken opposite sides, is really very much a question of words. We shall be pretty near the truth if we say that in the ecclesiastical courts before the Reformation the whole of the Canon Law, including the specially English Constitutions and Canons, was treated as *prima facie* authoritative; but that it was always recognized that Parliament, as representing the laity, could disallow or modify the operation within the realm of any part of this body of law, a right claimed likewise by the Governments of the great Continental States which professed a general obedience to the See of Rome."—*Church Quarterly Review*, Vol. LXV. p. 284.

form of specific change, or of long-continued disuse. Where some custom or ceremonial has been for a long time abandoned, the national Church must be assumed to have acquiesced in the disuse, and the claim by any individual to revive the ceremony or custom on his own initiative is inadmissible. For example, the Catholic rite of unction of the sick was never specifically prohibited in the English Church. Yet since for over three hundred years it has never been authoritatively recognized, the revival of it, which is greatly to be desired, must not come through the unauthorized action of individual clergy, but at least through Diocesan, if not indeed through Provincial action.

3. No colony may pass laws "repugnant to the laws of England." As every student of colonial history knows, this "repugnancy clause" has been the parent of many complicated legal questions. But the main principle is clear. There are certain principles embodied in imperial legislation that are intended to be binding on the whole Empire. For example, no colony may establish slavery or sanction torture, or refuse to recognize a discharge granted in British bankruptcy courts[1].

If any colony refuses to recognize these principles of legislation, it severs itself by that refusal from the life of the Empire. It loses all those undefinable, but most real, influences that belong to the life of a family

[1] Sir Henry Jenkyns, *British Rule and Jurisdiction beyond the Seas*, p. 6.

of nations held together in one organic whole by the bond of a common tradition, a common responsibility and a common hope.

The Christian society also has its catholic principles, which no national Church may change—its " One Lord, One Faith, One Baptism." But while there are courts that decide whether any given measure is repugnant to the laws of England, there is no court with the right to decide whether the laws of any national Church are repugnant to the laws of the catholic society. It is the desire for such a court that creates in minds of a certain type a strong leaning to the Roman system.

But if we cannot accept the verdict of the papacy as final on the question of what is catholic, are we left with no guidance ?

There is an obvious reply—it was the reply of the Reformers. The limits of the authority of national Churches are fixed by the Holy Scriptures, which are the common inheritance of all the Churches. But this is not, by itself, an adequate answer.

For the Bible is not a textbook of Canon law, but the record of the life-history of a great idea, till it becomes embodied in a society. The Bible appeals to a greater court behind itself. " There is One Body and One Spirit "—the One Spirit that abides for ever in the One body as the source and sustainer of its life. *Securus judicat orbis terrarum.* The instinct of the whole Christian society, where it is free to express itself, is the test of Catholicity. Where it is free to express itself—for the Christian society in any particular place may come under the control of political influences, and then it will tend to emphasize the sectional and national at the expense of the catholic; or it may come under the influence of a hieratical caste, and then it will tend to emphasize the catholic at the cost of the local and national. Or it may come under the control of influences that are both hieratical and political, and then the Christian conscience, stifled under the weight of counsels of opportunism, becomes unresponsive to the call of the Spirit, and "he that is prudent shall keep silence in such a time, for it is an evil time."

But, it may be asked, does this mean that we are to appeal from the trained expert and the learned theologian to the man in the street? And I would answer that it was exactly this that Christ did. His teaching was catholic because it dealt with the common needs, and appealed to the common instincts, of men. He founded an imperishable kingdom on the basis of belief in the essential soundness of the human conscience, and the essential goodness of the human heart. Of course I do not mean that ignorance is a necessary qualification for spiritual insight, or that there is no place in the Christian society for the scholar and the expert. But I do mean that the man whose ideas of

religion are based upon distrust of humanity will differ
entirely in his conception of the Church from the man
who believes that the human heart, when enlightened
by the Spirit of God, becomes subtly responsive to
truth in doctrine and reality in worship. For those
who hold the former view will be exercised to guard
against the intrusion of the layman into holy things;
they will conceive of education as successful in proportion as it trains up a body of men willing to accept
without question the dogmas of the Catholic Faith;
while those who hold the latter view will seek, like
S. Paul, to commend themselves to every man's conscience in the sight of God; they will recognize the
truth *Salus populi, suprema lex*—nothing is Catholic
to which the heart of the ordinary member of the
Christian society does not respond, when it is true to
itself; they will conceive of Christian education as,
above all else, the training of the conscience of the
individual, so that it may become a sensitive instrument
for registering the verdict of the Holy Spirit.

For after all, to return to the analogy that we were
considering, the imperial principles of legislation that
remain valid for every part of the Empire must ultimately depend for their validity on the fact that the
general opinion of the Empire recognizes their utility.
And so catholic law and custom can ultimately only
mean the law and custom that corresponds with the
needs of the human heart in all ages and nations.

We should therefore expect to find, as indeed is the case, that every national Church is almost completely free in regard to matters of custom and ceremonial[1]. True, we must not, in the words of Hooker, "lightly esteem what hath been allowed as fit in the judgment of antiquity, and by the long-continued practice of the whole Church; from which unnecessarily to swerve, experience hath never as yet found it safe." Yet "the Church" (and here Hooker means the Church of England) "hath authority to establish that for an order at one time, which at another it may abolish, and in both do well[2]."

The same claim is, as we all know, incorporated in our Thirty-fourth Article, and in the closing words of the statement *Of Ceremonies*, affixed by Cranmer to the first Prayer Book of Edward VI.

The principle on which this claim is based is the principle of Pentecost—the right of every nation to translate the message of God into its own language. For the catholic manhood of our Lord expressed itself in the outward forms of the Jewish life of the first century; and expresses itself again in the outward forms of the life of every nation that is made wise to interpret that life in the light of its own characteristics and needs.

---

[1] On this question see *The Right of Particular Churches in Matter of Practice*, by the Bishop of Gibraltar (Ch. Hist. Soc., Tract LXXXII.).

[2] Hooker, *Ecclesiastical Polity*, Bk v. ch. vii.

Ceremonial is part of the language in which a nation expresses its religious aspirations. And unless the language is its own, it is, to a large extent, useless. We may think of a catholic ceremonial, as we may think of an universal language, as an ideal about which we may dream if we will. But meanwhile we must speak the actual languages of men, or be content to remain unintelligible.

Perhaps, indeed, the very variety of human languages serves to keep us from forgetting the inadequacy of all human speech. The doctrine of the verbal inspiration of the Bible could not for long survive the translation of the Bible into all the varied languages of men; and as we have abandoned the idea of the verbal inspiration of the Scriptures, and gained immeasurably in real understanding of their message, so we shall before long abandon the idea of the verbal inspiration of the creeds. We shall love them not less but more as we come to feel in them the throb of human hearts feeling after words adequate to express the truths that are yet too large for language. It is not in any words of men, but only in the Word of God, that truth finds its adequate expression.

Language cannot fully express truth, nor ceremonial fully embody it. But the language of each nation, developing with the growth of national life, constantly testing and enrolling fresh recruits in its vocabulary, regulated in its growth not by law, but by the general instinct of the people, and the influence of the great literature of the past, becomes for each nation the most adequate vehicle for the expression of truth.

And as with language, so with ceremonial. Symbols that need to be explained, by that very fact prove that they have ceased to be of service. Ceremonial that is luminous in its native atmosphere may become "dumb and dark" when transplanted into a different environment. Even in the Holy Eucharist itself, part of the significance of the service is lost in a country where wine is not the common drink of the people.

Yet as the languages of Western Europe still indicate in their structure the influence of a common origin, so the ceremonial language of the Churches of the Christ may be expected to show, under all divergences of detail, a certain fundamental identity.

The degree to which divergence of custom may coexist with real identity of meaning may be illustrated by the case of Confirmation. The Roman Church confirms young people by episcopal Unction without the laying on of hands; the Eastern Church confirms infants by Unction administered by a priest with oil consecrated by the bishop ; the English Church confirms young people by laying on of hands without Unction. Yet all these Churches agree as to the nature of the gift conveyed in Confirmation. It is needless to multiply examples.

But by what process does a national Church translate the catholic truth into its own ceremonial language ? The language of a nation is being perpetually adapted by an almost unconscious process to the varying needs of national life. A great writer or speaker may give right of entry to some new word or phrase, or it may grow up almost, as it were, in secret, till it becomes current coin. But this is only possible in an atmosphere of freedom. Who would dream of committing the control of the development of the English language to a judicial court or a committee of experts ?

We know that freedom has its dangers ; that our English speech is liable to be corrupted by the vagaries and eccentricities of the moment ; that local dialects die hard. Yet we trust the future of our English speech to the English people, we leave in its keeping our thoughts and prayers. To every nation its own language ; this is ours ; the symbol of the soul of a people, the sacrament of a historic life that lives for a destiny beyond the present.

As with language, so with ceremonial. I would plead for the widest possible scope for experiment in the ceremonial of a national Church, for the frank abandonment of any attempt at a cast-iron system of legally enforced uniformity. With it must go too the arbitrary power of the clergy to modify and expand local uses in accordance with the supposed ceremonial of the Catholic Church. The experience of the colonial Churches has shown conclusively that the Christian laity, when entrusted with real power, are a strong safeguard against rash or ill-considered changes in the customs and ceremonial of the Church. But experiment and adaptation are only possible to a body that has an organic character. And it is this organic character that a national Church is best fitted to secure and retain. For the life of the Church is grafted on the foundation of the organic life of the nation[1].

A nation is an organism, even though the mass of the people seem dead to the throb of its organic life, though like an aged oak there flows through its battered trunk only so much of sap as shall renew in the spring-time the green of one solitary bough. So a national Church may still live though only a small minority of the nation is enrolled in the number of its active members. For a Church is not national merely because it includes a majority of the nation, but because it embodies the special contribution that the nation has to make to the religious life of the world. A Church ceases to be national in proportion as it ceases to

---

[1] "In every nation the universal mission of the Church must be fulfilled according to the peculiar circumstances of the national history and of the national character. And if the nation is, as we hold, a living whole, its constitution will be incomplete if it has no organ for the development and for the expression of its spiritual powers; if it has not, in other words, a national Church." Westcott, *Social Aspects of Christianity*, p. 76.

include within itself all the religious forces of the national life. It ceases to be a Church, in the sense in which I am using the word, in proportion as it ceases to reach out beyond the life of the nation into the life of humanity.

In S. Paul's view, the enrichment of the Christian society is brought about by the diversity of the gifts bestowed by the One Spirit on each man for the common good. So the whole Christian society is still enriched by the diverse gifts that the One Spirit has bestowed upon the nations, when these gifts are made available for the whole body through the Church life of each nation.

The time has surely come when we may hope for the synthesis of the two really fruitful conceptions of the Church that came into prominence in the century just past—the conception of a national Church associated with the names of Coleridge, Arnold and Stanley; and the conception of the Catholic Church that gave its strength to the Oxford movement. For both conceptions are true. It is true on the one hand that the Church cannot live as a disembodied ideal, unrelated to all the local associations that make up the actual life of men—that her mission can only be fulfilled in so far as she can become incarnate in the life of the people, and gather to herself all the forces of good that belong to the family, the tribe, the nation.

Yet it is true, on the other hand, that the local society lives, not for itself, but for humanity, that it draws its life from hidden fountains of strength, that it has "come unto mount Zion, and unto the city of the living God, the heavenly Jerusalem, and to innumerable hosts of angels, to the general assembly and Church of the first born, who are enrolled in heaven."

There is no real conflict between true patriotism and love for humanity, for all true patriotism is the embodiment in concrete form of the love that reaches out beyond the individual life in ever-widening circles of service [1]. And there is no conflict between the catholic and national conceptions of the Church, for every national Church is the embodiment in concrete form of the claim that the whole Christian society makes on the life of the individual. In loyalty to my city, and my nation, I can best serve humanity; in loyalty to the English Church, I can best serve that

[1] "The truly disinterested social life of a man who lives (not merely in and on his people, but) for his people, in whom the true civic or national spirit dominates over all purely personal and separate interests, may, analogously to the life of religion, be resolved into a sort of faith, charity and hope. For in such a man the general mind and outlook supplants the personal and private; the general ends, interests and affections absorb and transcend the particular; and as an active member of the social organism his internal and external energies are reinforced by those of the whole community which acts with him and through him." Tyrrell, *A Much Abused Letter*, p. 76.

Catholic Church, which exists in its completeness only in the mind of God, and, in its, as yet, imperfect human counterpart, includes every congregation of faithful men in which the pure word of God is preached, and the sacraments duly administered.

May I close by adapting the eloquent words of one not of our communion, who has suffered much through faithfulness to the truth as he sees it:

The English Church "may be no more than the charred stump of a tree torn to pieces by gales and rent by thunderbolts; she may be, and probably is, more responsible for all the schisms than the schismatics themselves, yet, unlike them, she stands for the principle of Catholicity, for the ideal of a spiritually united humanity centred round Christ in one divine society —of the Kingdom of God governed by the Son of God [1]."

"To belong to this world-wide, authentic, and original Christian society, to appropriate its universal life as far as possible, to be fired with its best enthusiasms, to devote oneself to its services and aims, is to go out of one's selfish littleness and to enter into the vast collective life—the hopes and fears, the joys and sorrows, failures and successes—of all those millions who have borne, or bear, or shall yet bear the name of Catholic, and who have in any degree lived worthy of that name [2]."

[1] Tyrrell, *A Much Abused Letter*, p. 77.   [2] *Ibid.* p. 64.

IV

CHURCH AND STATE.

S. MARK XII. 17.

*Render unto Cæsar the things that are Cæsar's, and
unto God the things that are God's.*

Divorced from their context, these words might be
taken to imply that there are two spheres of life that
the Christian man must keep carefully apart—that
Cæsar must not be allowed to intrude into the province
that belongs to God or God into the realm within which
Cæsar holds sway. But when we examine the words
in the light of their context, we see that their meaning
is exactly the opposite of this. For the question of
the Pharisees was practically this, Does our duty to
God oblige us to refuse recognition to the established
secular authority? And the reply of our Lord is that
the two duties must not be separated—that religion
and citizenship have both their appointed place in a
rightly ordered life. It lifts the obligation of con-
tributing to Imperial taxation into a new atmosphere by
associating it with the claim of God on the lives of men.

But when we try to apply the principle to the

actual problem of the relation of Church and State we are involved in complicated questions. For how is a man to decide in his own life what things are Cæsar's and what are God's? And if he must beware of giving to Cæsar what belongs to God, must he not also beware of the danger into which the Pharisees were falling, of claiming for God what belonged to Cæsar?

These considerations bring us face to face with the question of the relations of Church and State—the question that I ask you to consider in this last lecture.

At the outset, it is important to distinguish between the problem of the relation of the Church to the State and the problem of the relation of the Church to the nation. Ideally, the State is the nation organized for self-protection and self-development, just as ideally the Church is the nation organized for the work of service to humanity. But just as, in fact, the Church is not coextensive with the nation, so the State, as an actually effective body, consists only of a majority of the citizens, or even, under some constitutions, a minority. At any given moment, in this country, a considerable number of citizens, either through apathy or active opposition to the existing government, are "nonconforming[1]" members of the State. True, the nonconformity is not carried to the length of actual separation from the state life—partly

[1] The "Nonconformity" is of course only subjective, except in the case of "Passive resistance."

because the common basis of national interest is stronger than the disruptive tendencies, and partly because the coercive power of the State is exercised to repress any actual schism in the national organization. Any widespread refusal, for example, by those who objected to the policy of the government, to pay taxes, or, in countries that have adopted compulsory military service, to serve in the army, would be met by any modern State by an appeal to force. It is only under exceptional circumstances, and in an undemocratic State, that such a policy as that of Deák in Hungary before 1866 can hope to succeed.

I desire to lay some stress on this point, because it is important to recognize that if the English Church does not represent anything like an overwhelming majority of the nation, neither does the English State.

But here we notice a difference. The English State machinery falls into the control of the political party that, for the moment, has the majority of votes; but the control of the machinery of the English Church remains in the hands of the same body. In other words, in the State the "nonconforming" members of to-day may be the governing party of to-morrow; while in the Church, the nonconformist is, as it were, permanently in opposition.

The reason for this is obvious. By its nature, the Church is precluded from using those coercive powers by which the State prevents schism in the political life of the nation, and therefore that part of the nation that does not find itself in harmony with the existing order of things in the Church has abandoned the effort to mould the life of the English Church from within, and has formed voluntary religious societies for itself. In a word, the opposition in the State remains within the society, the opposition in the Church tends to go outside.

The Church and the State are alike in this, that in neither is the national life fully represented. But in the deeper issues of national life party spirit is forgotten and the State machine moves under the impulse of a General Will that lies behind the diverging interests on the surface of political life. So in the deeper issues of religious life there is a General Will, deeper than the prejudices and bitterness of the moment, of which the Church becomes almost unconsciously the exponent. Through a hundred subtle channels of influence, the English Church is affected by the thought and life of the other religious bodies in the nation. Its life is intertwined with theirs; they are not strengthened by its weakness, or impoverished by its wealth of spiritual life. If it could perish, who could dare to hope that voluntary religious societies, acknowledging no responsibility to the whole Christian society, committed to no obligation to maintain the traditions of an unbroken history, would prove strong enough to keep alive in the national life the undying witness to the one Truth that belongs to all the Churches of the Christ—the evidence of their common ancestry, the guarantee of their common destiny.

The State is the nation organized for the purpose of protecting its right to independence and self-expression. And therefore it is bound to exercise a certain measure of control over all voluntary societies within its area that are liable to endanger its existence. It must protect the moral basis of its own organized life. A religious body within the State that teaches disloyalty, or disregards the elementary principles of morality that the State regards as essential to its welfare, cannot claim immunity from State interference. The Roman Imperial government could not, till it became itself Christian, give toleration to a religion that set itself against the whole religious policy of the Empire. Nor, again, could the Elizabethan statesmen grant freedom of worship to the adherents of the old faith while that faith was, by the action of the Pope, identified with disloyalty to the crown. The government of the United States cannot recognize a religion that sanctions polygamy, or the Indian government acquiesce in the custom of *suttee*.

This right of interference becomes more defined when the religious body is in possession of property. For as the State guarantees the body in the corporate possession of its property, it must claim the right to see that it is not diverted to uses other than those for which it was originally intended. From this measure of State control no religious body can hope to be free, unless it has nothing that it can call its own.

And, undoubtedly, this is true in a special degree of a Church that is, in any sense, established. For property given to such a Church cannot be dissociated from its established character.

But if we ask what, exactly, is meant by establishment, the question is not easy to answer. There are established Churches in Russia, Greece, Prussia, Scandinavia, England, Scotland and Italy, but in no two of these countries does establishment take the same form. The clergy may be paid directly by the State, as in Italy and Norway, or from endowments and voluntary contributions, as in England, Scotland and Sweden, or by a combination of both, as in Russia. The Church may be under direct State control, as in Russia, or enjoy a varying measure of independence, as in Prussia, England, and Scotland. It may coexist with other bodies enjoying complete freedom of worship, as in England, or it may have a monopoly of public worship, as in Spain, and, practically, in Russia.

An established Church may perhaps be defined as a Church to which the State grants protection in the possession of property allocated to religious purposes, and a certain measure of official recognition; and which, in return, undertakes to provide the ministrations of religion freely to all in the nation who are willing to avail themselves of them[1].

Two questions arise out of this definition. 1. To what extent does this relation involve the interference of the State with the Church? and 2. Is the relation itself in the best interest of the State and the Church?

With regard to the first of these, it is obvious that the State must have the right to take such steps as shall insure that the implied contract is fulfilled. It has a just ground for interference if the Church does not bring its services and sacraments within reach of the people. And it has just ground for interference if the religion that is brought to the people is not the religion that the Church has contracted to supply. No one doubts, for example, that if the English Church were formally to repudiate any fundamental doctrine of the Christian faith, the State would be within its rights in withdrawing its recognition, and even in transferring the endowments of the Church to some

[1] " Wherever we have a certain legal provision for the ministrations of Christianity, there we have an establishment of Christianity in the land. It is this which forms the essence of establishment." Dr Chalmers, *Lectures on the Establishment and Extension of National Churches*, Lect. 6.

" The division of the country into districts, and the stationing in each district a teacher of religion, forms the substantial part in every Church establishment. The varieties that have been introduced into the government and discipline of different Churches are of inferior importance when compared with this, in which they all agree." Paley, *Moral and Political Philosophy*, Bk. VI. ch. X.

other body willing to minister to the religious needs of the people.

How far that right extends is, of course, a matter for discussion. It might be so exercised, and indeed is so exercised at present[1], as to deprive the Church of that right to development that must belong to every corporate body that has a continuing life. But this is not of the essence of establishment, and a recent decision of the House of Lords has shown that Free Churches are not free from the same danger of being stunted in their development by the pedantries of legal interpretation.

It is the duty of the State to protect the right of

[1] " We have long rid ourselves of all the secular burdens imposed by what we call the Tudor dictatorship, but we are still living under religious or ecclesiastical conditions that owe very much, even in their present form, to the hand of Henry." Stubbs, *Lectures on Mediaeval and Modern History*, p. 262.

I have intentionally refrained from entering into any detailed consideration of the question of self-government in the English Church. The example of the Established Church of Scotland shows that it is possible for a Church to be established and yet free from the galling restrictions that historical circumstances have imposed upon the Church of England. The one essential condition of any attempt to restore self-government in the English Church is that the power of the laity shall be a reality and not a sham. Limited and carefully restricted powers, conceded to the laity by clergy intrenched in state-protected freeholds, can hardly be expected to evoke any enthusiastic response from the general body of Churchmen. On the position of the laity in the early Church see Westcott, *Lessons from Work*, p. 422 ff. ; also Essay by the Rev. R. B. Rackham in *Essays in aid of the Reform of the Church* (Murray, 1902).

the layman to the sacraments and services of the Church on the conditions defined in the constitution of the Church or in documents to which the Church has given its sanction. Every English child has the right to be baptized into membership of the Christian society; every adult confirmed person has the right to a place at the Church's altar unless excommunicated by episcopal authority; every parishioner has the right to free access to his parish Church and to the provision of daily services therein, and a sermon every Sunday. And the State has the right to see that the Church does what she has specifically agreed to do.

In all this, there is nothing to which the most scrupulous Churchman can reasonably object. He cannot complain that his Church is asked to give security for her faithfulness to her own avowed principles. She is not justified in appealing to Catholic principles for protection against obligations to which she has assented, and in virtue of which she holds her place in the national life[1].

[1] "If I would keep up the Established Church of England, it is not for the sake of lords and baronets, and country gentlemen of £5000 a year and rich bankers in the city. I know that such people will always have Churches, aye, and Cathedrals, and organs and rich communion plate. The person for whom I am uneasy is the working man; the man who would find it difficult to pay 5*s.* or even 10*s.* a year out of his small earnings for the ministrations of religion. What is to become of him under the voluntary system? Is he to go without religious instruction altogether? That we should all think a great evil to himself and a great evil to society? Is he to pay for it

The true way to minimize the interference of the State is not an appeal to Catholic tradition, but a fuller application of that Catholic principle that gives to the general consent of the Christian society an effective control over the executive organ. The more clearly the nation's voice is heard within the Church, the less will it menace her from without. A Church that dares to trust the people will have no need to stand on guard against the interferences of the State.

And if the Church is, as I have tried to show, fundamentally democratic in its divinely appointed constitution, it should find itself peculiarly at home in the life of a nation that is self-governing and democratic. If it is the enemy of privilege and irresponsible wealth, and the friend of the poor and the meek; if under its robe, stained and torn with the conflicts of ages, there beats still the child-like heart that trusts and hopes, it cannot find itself a stranger and an alien in the world of common men.

But there remains the question, Is this relation

out of his slender means? That would be a heavy tax. Is he to be dependent on the liberality of others? That is a somewhat precarious and a somewhat humiliating dependence. I prefer, I own, that system under which there is, in the rudest and most secluded districts, a house of God, where public worship is performed after a manner acceptable to the great majority of the community, and where the poorest may partake of the ordinances of religion, not as an alms, but as a right." Macaulay, *Speech on Maynooth College Grant*, 1845.

between the Church and the State in the best interest of both ?

Establishment has been defended by English writers at different times on very varying grounds. The doctrine of the Reformers, as represented by the work of their great exponent Hooker, lays stress on the " pattern of God's ancient people[1]," and finds a justification for the Royal Supremacy in the prerogative "given always to all Godly Princes in Holy Scriptures by God Himself." This identification of Church and nation, in the supposed interests of the former, ceased to be possible as soon as nonconformity secured a recognized position in national life, and is practically abandoned by Thorndike, the ablest exponent of the doctrine of an established Church in the Restoration period.

In the eighteenth century Warburton, in his *Alliance between Church and State*, bases his whole contention on the essential separateness of Church and State, the State being occupied with the care of the body, the Church with the care of the soul. In view of the actual condition of the Church in England in the early part of the eighteenth century,

[1] "With us one society is both the Church and Commonwealth, which with them (the early Christians) it was not.......In a word, our estate is according to the pattern of God's own ancient elect people, which people was not part of them the Commonwealth and part of them the Church of God, but the self-same people whole and entire were both under one chief governor, on whose supreme authority they did all depend." Hooker, *Ecclesiastical Polity*, Bk. VIII. ch. i.

Warburton's complaisant optimism is not easy to understand. He defends establishment on grounds of "civil utility," and shares Burke's enthusiasm for the existing system[1].

Coleridge, though apparently simplifying the question by introducing a new distinction between the national Church and the Christian Church, in reality only complicates it. For now there are two Churches, a national Church, only accidentally Christian, within the State, and a Christian Church outside it. As a kind of glorified Board of Education, the national Church is to direct the intellectual and moral progress of the nation. It should also "afford every opportunity and present no obstacle to a gradual advancement of the Church of Christ." But this national Church is a fiction, of which history knows nothing. The religious consciousness of the nations of Europe has organized itself on a Christian basis. A national religion only accidentally Christian has never yet found a place in any civilized community, and though, as I have already said (see p. 27), some modern thinkers have been drawn to the idea as a way of escape from our present educational entanglements, any attempt to carry it out

---

[1] "From all this it will appear, which is one of the principal purposes of this discourse, that our present happy constitution, both of Church and State, is erected on solid and lasting foundations." *Alliance between Church and State.* He did, however, recognize that Convocation was not sufficiently free from State control.

could only end in the establishment of a state religion liable to changes as constant and perplexing as the changes of our present educational department, and the isolation of the Christian Church as an alien body in the national life.

Mr Gladstone's treatise on *The State in its relations with the Church* is not inaptly described by Macaulay as "the strenuous effort of a very vigorous mind to keep as far in the rear of the general progress as possible."

To Mr Gladstone's contention that the State should propagate the true religion it may be replied that the State can only act within the limits of the purpose for which it exists. Whole departments of life lie outside its province. In as far as the nation is Christian, that Christianity may be expected to find expression in the policy of the State. But the State cannot act in advance of the general mind of the people; it cannot propagate religion, for what the State enjoins it must enforce, if not by direct coercion, at least by such indirect coercion as shall penalize the recalcitrant. And religion must not be propagated by coercion.

Macaulay, in his Essay on Mr Gladstone's volume, by defining the main end of government as "the protection of persons and property," relegates the instruction of the people to a subordinate place in the programme of the State, and so leaves a large area free for the activities of the Church, under such measure of State control as expediency may dictate.

I have only examined these earlier attempts to defend establishment to show how the circumstances of modern life, while leaving the fact of establishment in this country, have decreased, or even destroyed, the value of the arguments by which earlier advocates defended it. Are we then to decide that the entire separation of Church and State is the true ideal?

To this it may be replied, that the claims of Cæsar and of God cannot thus be separated without loss. In the personal life of the Christian the attempt to separate religion and citizenship reacts disastrously on both. His religion becomes in danger of degenerating into a selfish quest for personal salvation; his citizenship is deprived of the inspiration that can only come from a creed that claims every human life for the common good in the Name of Him who laid down His life for the ignorant and the sinful in the passion of self-forgetful love.

But if true citizenship needs the inspiration of a religious motive, it cannot be the wisdom of the State to make no provision for its own education in that for lack of which its life must be impoverished and mean. It must not force religion on its citizens or penalize those who refuse to accept the Christian creed. The days of state-enforced uniformity are gone, thank God, for ever, in lands that understand the meaning of liberty. But it may say, "Here is an ideal of life that came into the world nineteen hundred years ago. It has proved strong to resist the disintegrating influences of time; it has uplifted the nations that have made it, in any degree, their own. It is the ideal of an universal brotherhood expressed in the organic life of a great society that claims to be bound in sacramental union with the unnumbered generations of faithful men who have served God both in Church and State. It is not our function to examine its credentials or pronounce judgment on its claims, but we welcome the inspiration that it can give, we provide for every man the right to hear its gospel and be baptized into its membership. He may reject the gospel, and repudiate the membership; he may find in some other religious society fuller scope for his religious life; but he shall not lose his right to be served by the great society in so far as he is willing that it should serve him."

The Christian instinct cannot acquiesce in the idea of the State as a merely secular organization. For when we apply the word "secular" to any organization, what we mean is that it is an organization primarily concerned with the present and the material. But the nation, organized for the defence of its right to be, is primarily concerned with the perpetuation of a spiritual idea (see p. 11); and a State can only hope to maintain itself in proportion as it is willing to subordinate the present to the future—the mess of pottage to the birthright yet to be realized. It is exactly this spiritual character of the State that gives it the right to exercise a coercive power that it rightly denies to other forms of organized life within the nation.

Even if we conceive of the objects of the State as limited to "the protection of persons and property," it is obvious that this task will lead it into the region of moral ideas. The State cannot punish an errand boy for stealing apples without being confronted with moral problems of human character, the issues of which reach out into eternity[1]. The same instinct that led the early Church to lift the body as well as the soul into the sphere of redemption, repudiates the false spirituality that severs the things of Cæsar from the things of God. Impatience of the restraints that the body imposes on the soul's life might lead Gnostic or Manichee to

> bring the invisible full into play,
> Let the visible go to the dogs—what matters?

[1] "Every Society, every Polity, has a spiritual principle ; is the embodiment, tentative and more or less complete, of an Idea : all its tendencies of endeavour, specialties of custom, its laws, politics and whole procedure—are prescribed by an Idea and flow naturally from it, as movements from the living source of motion. This Idea,...has in it something of a religious, paramount, quite infinite character ; it is properly the Soul of the State, its life ; mysterious as other forms of life, and like these working secretly, and in a depth beyond that of consciousness." Thomas Carlyle.

But the sounder instinct of the Christian society read otherwise the lesson of the Incarnation, and ended its creed with an assertion of its belief in the eternal significance of the physical life of man. In its sacraments it linked the Divine presence with the common things of life, in its teaching it set forth a Kingdom of God that should include all human life under its sway.

For as the body has need of the soul that its life may be guided by intelligent purpose to noble ends, so not less the soul has need of the body as its instrument for service and self-expression. Body and soul are God's gift to each other. Together they grow under the shaping hands of God, together they fulfil their appointed work in the world. And though death severs the link that makes them one, the ultimate ideal to which the Christian man looks forward is the reunion of both in the fuller harmony of perfect service.

Does it seem too fanciful a thought that when the last of the prophets saw the new Jerusalem coming down from God out of heaven, and pictured the eternal world as a city having gates and walls, he thought of human citizenship as corresponding to some unimaginable reality in eternal things, as the body of our humiliation corresponds to the body of His glory?

Let us look at the same problem from another

point of view. A nation, like an individual, has two fundamental rights that it instinctively claims—the right to exist as an independent self-governing entity, and the right to link itself in bonds of mutual service with the whole life of humanity, not of the present only, but of the past and the future. Every man, every nation, desires to live and to love.

Out of the first of these desires grows the organized life of the State, claiming, should need arise, complete control over the life of the individual in the cause of the whole society; and to meet the second comes in the organized life of the Church, consecrating the instinct of self-protection by interpreting its meaning, counteracting the tendency to selfish isolation by her larger Catholic message, claiming the life of the individual as hers for service. Surely it is clear that the separation of these two claims cannot be the true ideal of national life.

We cannot now advocate the recognition of the Church by the State on the ground that the functions of the two are so diverse that each is necessary to complete the other. For exactly the opposite is now true. In every department of life and work the frontier lines of the Church and of the State intersect. In the school and the workshop, in the casual ward and the hospital—wherever ignorance or poverty or sickness or crime is found, there the Church and the State find themselves face to face—colleagues or rivals.

The Church cannot hope, even if it wished, to arrest this extension of the functions of the State. Unless it is prepared to be pushed slowly out of relation to the practical activities of life, it must abandon the idea of attempting to mark out spheres of influence, and ask itself whether its aims and those of the State are not capable of reconciliation. Perhaps we can best express the difference by saying that the end of the State is the preservation of the national life, and that it cares for the development of the character of the individual as a means to that end; whereas the end of the Church is the development of the character of the individual—his training for eternity—and that it cares for the preservation of the national life as a means to that end. If the need arise, the State will sacrifice the development—even the life—of the individual to the preservation of the life of the nation; while the Church—if it is true to itself—will rather choose that the nation shall perish than that it should be saved at the expense of moral character. By the recognition of the Church, the State provides the best safeguard for its own moral character; by the acceptance of that recognition, the Church asserts its belief that the true interest of the nation depends on the moral character of the individuals that compose it.

But there is one objection that we must not ignore. It is said that the abolition of all religious tests for membership of Parliament has, in England at least, profoundly changed the whole position. This is true. But though Parliament no longer speaks as a body of lay members of the Church, yet it does speak as, in some degree, the organ of the national life. It does, while it has the right to discuss Church questions, voice the prejudices and opinions, the desires and aspirations, of the nation. And these we cannot ignore. For a national Church must be sensitive to the currents of thought of the national life, it must learn to hear as well as to speak, to be taught as well as to teach. It must listen patiently to the critic as well as the eulogist. It must be willing to concede much, if it can keep that which is essential to its life. It must remember that its glory is in service, and that the Body of Christ must still be given for the life of the world.

For what, after all, is it that we ask when we ask that our position as an established Church shall not be taken from us ? It is easy to represent the demand as a mere clamour for endowments or privilege, for the highest seats in the synagogues, and the best rooms at the feasts. But we do not care for these things ; they are the accidents of history, and must perish.

No. What we ask for is the recognition of our right to serve the life of the nation, not merely as individuals but as a corporate body ; for the right to consecrate every English child at our fonts to the great task of service; for the right to kneel by every English deathbed to give back to God the nation's tired men and women when life's task is done; for the right to thank God for all His English servants departed this life in His faith and fear; for the right to make this England of ours a nation that shall not be ashamed to stand at the judgment bar of the Son of Man. There is danger lest we grow petulant and impatient under the restrictions imposed upon us by the task of service, lest we rashly clamour for a freedom of which we have not counted the cost. It is easy to say, "Let us go free." It is harder, and better, to say, "Give us[1] still the right to serve you. If we must serve in fetters that cripple and confine us, we will try to bear and be patient till you learn to know us better and trust us more fully." For the first claim of the Church of Christ is not the right to be independent, but the right to be the servant of all, "Even as the Son of Man came not to be served but to serve and to give His life a ransom for many."

For humanity is arranged in concentric circles of service. The clergy are the servants of the Church, the Church is the servant of the nation, the nation is

---

[1] It is perhaps necessary to say that "us" here does not mean the clergy but the whole body of faithful members of the English Church. A Church that leaves the task of service to the clergy is false to its fundamental principles. See Eph. iv. 12, where the work of the clergy is defined as "the equipping of the saints for the work of service" (πρὸς τὸν καταρτισμὸν τῶν ἁγίων εἰς ἔργον διακονίας).

the servant of humanity[1]. And from the centre of this circle, proceeding from the throne of God and of the Lamb, the Holy Spirit flows forth through every channel of service, making glad the City of God, where " His servants shall serve Him, and they shall see His face, and His name shall be in their foreheads."

[1] When Périer said "French blood belongs only to France"; Louis Blanc would reply, "Impious words! The genius of France has ever consisted in her cosmopolitanism, and self-sacrifice has been imposed on her by God equally as an element of her might and a condition of her existence." Andrews, *Historical Development of Modern Europe*, p. 305.

INDEX.